The Kids' Career Library™

A Day in the Life of a
Dancer

Helen C. Packard

The Rosen Publishing Group's
PowerKids Press™
New York

For Cleary

Published in 1997 by The Rosen Publishing Group, Inc.
29 East 21st Street, New York, NY 10010

First Edition

Book Design: Erin McKenna

Photo Illustrations: Cover and photo illustrations pp. 4, 11, 12, 15, 16, 19, 20 by Seth Dinnerman; p. 7 © Mark Newman/International Stock; p. 8 by Barnaby Shapiro.

Packard, Helen C.
    A day in the life of a dancer/ by Helen C. Packard.
        p.   cm. — (Kid's career library)
    Includes index.
    Summary: Presents the training and dedication necessary to be a dancer by describing the life of a modern dancer.
    ISBN 0-8239-5098-0
    1. Dance—Juvenile literature. 2. Dancers—Juvenile literature. [1. Dance. 2. Dancers.] I. Title. II. Series.
GV1596.5.P33 1997
792.8—dc21
                                                                        97-13940
                                                                            CIP
                                                                            AC

Manufactured in the United States of America

Contents

1 Expressing Herself   5

2 Starting Young   6

3 More Chances to Dance   9

4 Hard Work   10

5 S-T-R-E-T-C-H   13

6 New Projects   14

7 Working Together   17

8 Keeping Her Body Healthy   18

9 Showtime   21

10 Dancing Is Important   22

   Glossary   23

   Index   24

Expressing Herself

Brooke is a dancer. She dances with a **company** (KUM-puh-nee) called the Dance Aura Company.

Some people express their thoughts and feelings by writing books or poems. Others sing songs or play musical instruments. Brooke expresses herself through dance. She works with talented dancers and **choreographers** (KOR-ee-OG-ruh-ferz). Together they come up with movements that **interpret** (int-TER-pret) the ideas of the choreographer and express what Brooke is thinking and feeling.

◀ Brooke uses dancing as a way to communicate with other people.

5

Starting Young

Brooke started dancing when she was five years old. She took lessons in modern dance. In her classes, Brooke learned the basic skills she would use as a professional dancer. When she was older, she took lessons in different kinds of dance, such as jazz, ballet, African, and **flamenco** (fluh-MEN-coh).

Brooke's muscles grew stronger and she learned more about how her body moved. She learned that if she wanted to be a good dancer, she had to be **dedicated** (DED-ih-kay-ted), which meant she had to practice a lot.

6

Many children start dance classes when they are young, just like Brooke did. ▶

More Chances to Dance

In high school and college, Brooke **competed** (kum-PEET-ed) on dance teams. The teams also danced at sports events during the halftime break.

In college, Brooke took more dance classes. She learned from famous dance teachers who taught their own **techniques** (tek-NEEKS). She also danced with a college dance company in many **performances** (per-FOR-men-sez). She and the company performed for audiences of families, professors, students, and others.

◄ Some of Brooke's dances tell stories to the audience.

Hard Work

Brooke has fun dancing. But dancing requires a lot of hard work. Brooke takes classes almost every day.

Brooke works hard in other ways too. Dancing doesn't pay very much. So Brooke works as a waitress in a restaurant. Sometimes she teaches dance classes to children too. Doing so many jobs can be tiring. But Brooke knows that all the hard work is worth it. Having different jobs allows Brooke to do what she loves most—dance.

Brooke usually takes the bus or subway to her classes. But sometimes, if she is late, she takes a taxi. ▶

S-T-R-E-T-C-H

As a dancer, Brooke uses all the parts of her body. One of the most important things a dancer must do is to warm up and stretch all those body parts. Stretching muscles makes them more **flexible** (FLEX-ih-bul). When Brooke's body is warmed up, it is easier for her to dance well. Warming up and stretching also help keep Brooke's muscles from getting hurt during class. Brooke stretches at the *barre* (BAR) before and after every class.

◀ Brooke stretches the muscles in her legs and back at the *barre*.

13

New Projects

Brooke is always thinking of new ideas for dances. On some afternoons, Brooke and her friend Jessica eat lunch together and talk about their dancing and the performances of their company. Each performance tells a story or expresses an idea. A dance can be about anything. In one dance, the company told the story of students in China who were killed because they disagreed with their government.

Brooke and Jessica work hard to create a performance that will tell the audience what they think about a certain subject. ▶

Working Together

After lunch, Brooke works with everyone in the Dance Aura Company. First, the dancers work with a choreographer, who shares her ideas about a dance. Then the dancers add some of their own movements. Soon they are working together to combine these movements into a dance that **reflects** (ree-FLEKTS) the choreographer's ideas. It takes a lot of patience and **concentration** (kon-sen-TRAY-shun) to learn all the parts that go into a dance. A dance can take from six weeks to five months to complete.

◀ By practicing together almost everyday, the dancers learn a lot about each other and often become close friends.

17

Keeping Her Body Healthy

It's very important for a dancer to take care of his or her body. A healthy body helps a dancer stay strong and flexible. To stay healthy, Brooke tries to get a good night's sleep every night. Sometimes she takes naps during the day too. She also takes **yoga** (YOH-guh) classes once a week. Yoga helps Brooke to relax and stay flexible.

Eating healthy foods is important too. Fruit and vegetables give Brooke energy. She also drinks a lot of water. Water helps all of the systems in her body to work their best.

In yoga, this position is called a "bow." It helps Brooke strengthen her muscles and relax her mind. ▶

Showtime

One of Brooke's favorite parts of being a dancer is performing for an audience. On the day of a performance, she spends some quiet time by herself so she can be relaxed and feel good for the show. Then Brooke goes to the dressing room. She puts on makeup and fixes her hair. She puts on her costume and begins to stretch. Before showtime, the company practices the dance one more time. Everyone is excited. But Brooke still gets nervous before every performance!

◀ Being nervous before a show is okay. In fact, it helps Brooke to dance her best.

Dancing Is Important

Dancing is very important to Brooke. It is one way she can share part of herself with other people. She has learned that hard work and dedication are needed to become a successful dancer.

Brooke has also made some good friends in the dance company. The dancers in the company trust each other and rely on each other to do their best when they work together as a team. Being a dancer takes lots of energy. But it's exciting and fun. Brooke can't imagine being anything else!

Glossary

barre (BAR) The French word for a thin bar that is used for stretching and for different exercises.

choreographer (KOR-ee-OG-ruh-fer) A person who creates and directs the movements of a dance.

concentration (kon-sen-TRAY-shun) Paying close attention to something.

company (KUM-puh-nee) A group of people joined together for a common goal.

compete (kum-PEET) To try to win at something.

dedicate (DED-ih-kayt) To devote yourself to something.

flamenco (fluh-MEN-coh) A type of Spanish dancing.

flexible (FLEX-ih-bul) Able to move in many different ways.

interpret (in-TER-pret) To bring out and explain the meaning of something.

performance (per-FOR-ments) A show that is put on for others to watch.

reflect (ree-FLEKT) To show or express a thought.

technique (tek-NEEK) One's own way of doing something.

yoga (YOH-guh) A system of exercises that gives a person control and well-being over his or her mind and body.

23

Index

A
African dance, 6
audience, 9, 21

B
ballet, 6
barre, 13

C
choreographer, 5, 17
company, 5, 9, 14, 17, 21, 22
concentration, 17

D
Dance Aura Company, 5, 17
dedication, 6, 22

F
flamenco, 6
flexible, being, 13, 18

J
jazz, 6

M
modern dance, 6
muscles, 6, 13

P
performance, 9, 14, 21
practice, 6

S
stretching, 13

T
techniques, 9

Y
yoga, 18